CHROMOSOME KIDS LIKE ME

By Annette Fournier
Illustrated by Kelsey McKay

www.annettefournier.com
© 2018 Annette Fournier
All rights reserved. No portion of this book may be reproduced in any form without permission from the publisher, except as permitted by U.S. copyright law.
For permissions contact:
info@annettefournier.com
ISBN-13: 978-1718986299

Imprint: Independently published

Dedicated to my "Chromosome Kid", our "Chromosome 8 family" and to all the special people who were made a little bit differently.

Special thanks to Dr. Volkan Okur, Medical Geneticist at Columbia University, for his assistance.

Did you know we all have something called DNA?
It tells your body what to do, how to work, how to play.
DNA is in our bodies and the place it calls home,
are tiny little things called chromosomes.

Most people have 46 chromosomes, you see.
They're all matched up in pairs to make 23.
To make your body work, chromosomes are the key,
but they're just a little different in kids like me.

Not everyone's chromosomes make matching pairs.
Some are made differently, although it is rare.
Do you understand? Hmm, let me say what I want to explain in another way.

Imagine you have 23 pairs of socks.
They could be white or black or have polka dots.
The socks all match up, two by two.
At least that's what they usually do.

But imagine when you are putting on
your shoes,
you notice your socks are a little confused.
One sock is too long or too short
on one end,
or missing some parts in the middle, my
friend.

Maybe your sock was sewn top to toe,
so it looks like a little round ring or an O.
Sometimes you'll find there's just
one sock for you,
or perhaps your sock pair has three and not
two.

Maybe your socks decided to swap
the top for the bottom and the bottom
for the top.
Or two pairs combined to make something
new,
so the sock is mixed up, half red and half
blue.

So you know about socks, I have no doubt,
but chromosomes is what we were talking
about.
They can mix and match in ways that may
be,
just a little bit different in kids like me.

Sometimes chromosomes circle to
make an O,
or some people are missing one
you know.
Some pairs have three chromosomes rather
than two,
Some people's go together in a way that is
new.

Some parts are cut short and some parts are
cut long,
Some pieces are added that don't usually
belong.
Some chromosomes are short and some
are big.
Sometimes they zag when they
usually zig.

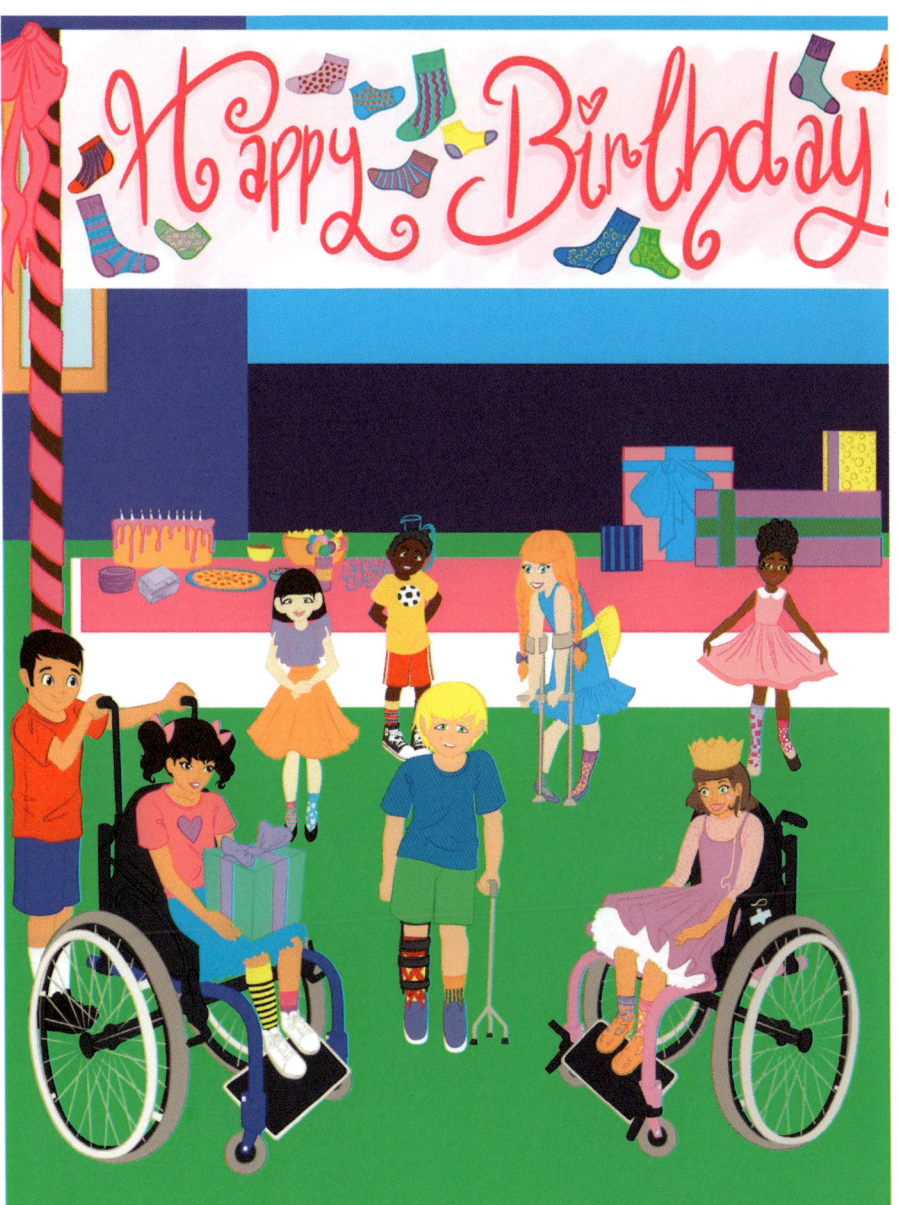

So what does it matter if our chromosomes pairs,
are a little bit different from his, her or theirs?
I will tell you if you listen with care,
because chromosome kids are a little bit rare.

Kids like me might do things that seem unique.
Our muscles might be extra tight or more weak.
We might be a little slower to think,
or to learn how to talk or to walk or to drink.

We might need extra help with the things that we do,
like playing with friends or tying a shoe.
Do you think you could help us? I think that you could.
Kind people help others and helping is good.

And when you help others I think you will find,
it makes you feel good inside to be kind.
Someday you may find that you need help too,
and maybe that day, I could come and help you.

No matter your abilities, the things you can do,
you are special just because you are you.
And that's true of chromosome kids like me.
We are not very different at all, you see.

So remember now as we come to the end,
I'm just a person like you and we can be friends.
When it comes right down to it we know through and through,
we're amazing the way we are, both me and you.

Authors Note:

Genetics is the study of DNA and chromosomes. DNA is like an instruction manual that tells our bodies how to work. DNA is bundled up into little packages called chromosomes that are inside the cells in our bodies.

Doctors and scientists study genetics to understand how chromosomes and genes work. Most people have 46 chromosomes, and they usually come in pairs. Those pairs are numbered from 1 to 22. The last pair is represented by X and Y. Usually, females have XX and males have XY.

However some people's chromosomes are made a little differently. They might be missing pieces, have extra pieces, be mixed together or have other differences. Chromosome differences can affect how a person's body and brain function or have very little or no effect. In fact, some people have chromosome differences and don't even know they have them!

When someone's chromosomes are different, doctors call it a "chromosome abnormality" or a "chromosome disorder". Chromosome disorders can be very complicated and some people have more than one disorder.

Here are a few types of chromosome disorders.

1. Trisomy - Trisomy is when someone has an extra copy of part or a whole chromosome so they have 47 instead of 46. People with Down syndrome have an extra copy of chromosome 21. Sometimes Down syndrome is called Trisomy 21.

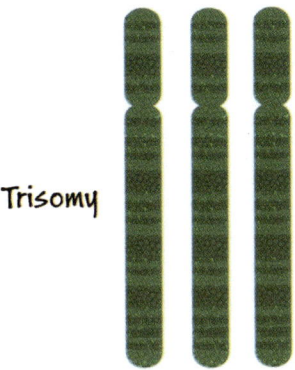

Trisomy

2. Monosomy - Monosomy is when a person is missing a chromosome, so they have 45 instead of 46. Except for mosaicism, the only people with 45 chromosomes are girls with Turner Syndrome. They have one X chromosome instead of two.

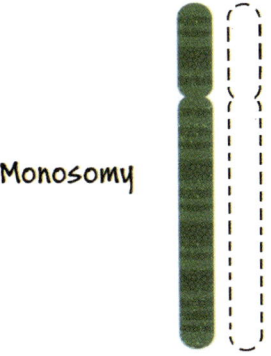

Monosomy

3. Duplication – A duplication is when part of a chromosome copies itself, so that the chromosome has twice as much of some DNA as is typical.

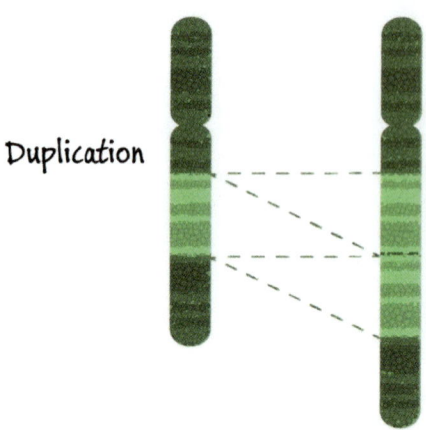

4. Deletion – A deletion is when part of a chromosome is missing. Chromosome deletions cause some conditions such as Cri du chat.

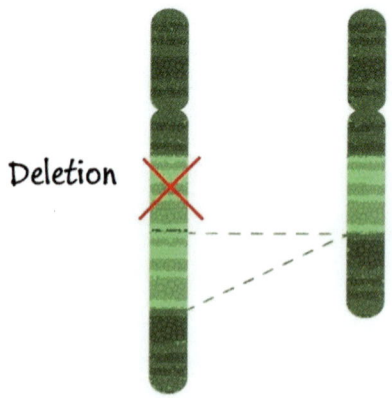

5. Inversion – An inversion is when part of a chromosome is flipped upside down. Sometimes inversions cause problems, and sometimes they don't seem to cause any problems. Some people have inversions and don't even know it!

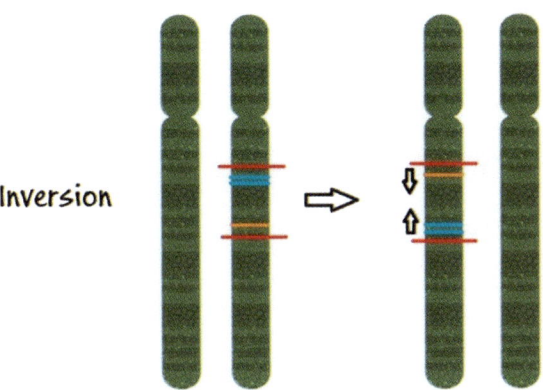
Inversion

6. Ring - Chromosomes are usually shaped like a line, but sometimes the two ends connect to form a ring. Often the ends of the chromosome are deleted before the ends stick together.

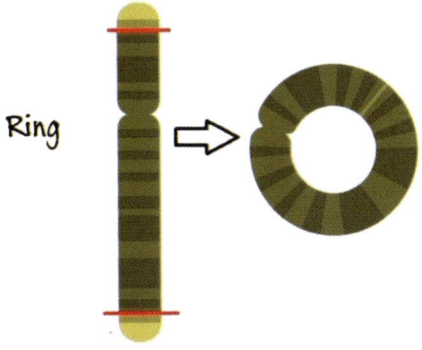
Ring

7. Translocation- A translocation is when a piece of one chromosome detaches and attaches itself to a different chromosome.

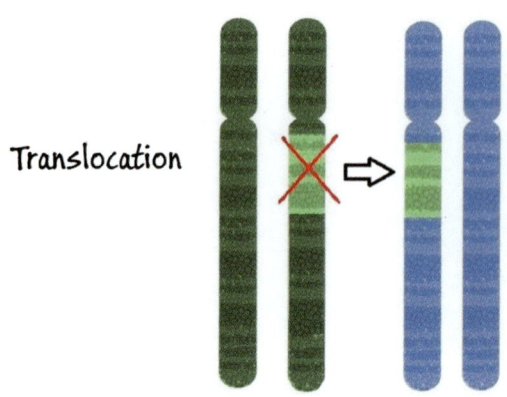

Translocation

8. Mosaicism – People with mosaicism have a mix of cells that are typical or "normal", and cells that are not typical. For instance, a person with mosaicism of Trisomy 21 has some cells that have 46 chromosomes and some cells that have 47 chromosomes. The greater number of abnormal cells they have, the more impaired they will be.

9. A little more information: Chromosomes are divided into two halves called p and q. Doctors call the short half "p" and the longer half "q". Do you want to know why they are called p and q? P stands for "petite" because the p arm is smaller. Q doesn't stand for anything! It just comes after p in the alphabet!

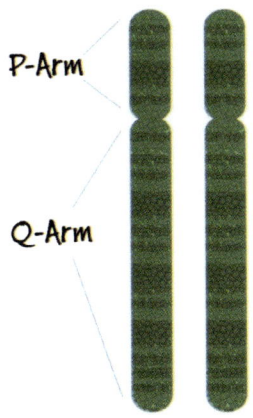

Sometimes you may hear about a chromosome disorder that has a number and the letter p or q. The letter tells you where on the chromosome the difference is located. Now if someone tells you the name of a chromosome disorder, you will be able to understand what it means! When we understand something that helps us know it is not weird or mysterious at all.

People with chromosome disorders have some small changes in the way they were made, but they're still wonderful, special people, just like you!

Printed in Great Britain
by Amazon